Developing Leaders

Training for small group leaders

*E*mpowering
*P*eople

Empowering
People

Other titles in this series:

Empowering People
Help! I am leading part of my Small Group
Small Groups—an Introduction
Encounter—20 Interactive Bible Studies for Small Groups

Developing Leaders

Copyright © Laurence Singlehurst and Trevor Withers 2018
The right of Laurence Singlehurst and Trevor Withers to be identified as authors this work has been asserted by them in accordance with the Copyright, Designs and Patents Act 1988

Excerpt from *'The Challenge of Cell Church'* used by kind permission of Phil Potter

Published and distributed by:

Cell UK Ministries,
Highfield Oval,
Harpenden, Herts.
AL5 4BX

First published in the UK in 2018

All Scripture quotations, unless otherwise indicated, are from the Holy Bible, New International Version®, NIV® Copyright ©1973, 1978, 1984, 2011 by Biblica, Inc.® Used by permission. All rights reserved worldwide.

ISBN: 978-1-902144-54-2   E&OE

Contents

		Page
Introduction		4
Chapter 1	Beliefs	7
Chapter 2	Values	15
Chapter 3	Where do small groups fit?	25
Chapter 4	Using the bible in our small groups	31
Something to discuss - an introduction		38
Chapter 5	Group dynamics	39
Chapter 6	Supporting small group leaders	53
Chapter 7	Small group evangelism	63
Chapter 8	Experiencing life in a small group	77
Other resources		91
About the authors		94

Introduction

'I continue to dream and pray about a revival of holiness in our day that moves forth in mission and creates authentic community in which each person can be unleashed through the empowerment of the Spirit to fulfil God's creational intentions.'

So speaks John Wesley. His words are as relevant today as they were when he first wrote them. He saw something of his prayers answered as his movement of small groups known as classes empowered and transformed the lives of those who attended them. This in turn spilled out into the lives of these faithful people and turned the country upside down for God's kingdom.

The need for small group leaders

There is no doubt that many of our churches would benefit from having more small groups to encourage a sense of Christian community where we disciple and support each other to help us live out our faith in everyday life. Often the challenge is not a shortage of people wanting to be in these groups but rather those who are able to lead them. Over the last 20 years or so, we have had the privilege of seeing leaders raised up and trained to effectively lead vibrant small groups. We have done this working with churches from different streams and denominations up and down the country.

The key to success here has been the priority that churches have given to running regular training opportunities where the theory and practice of good small group leadership come together. What we have found is that what we describe as 'light leadership' means that the role is less burdensome making longer term leadership more sustainable and creating greater ownership by those who are members of the group.

This booklet has been designed to enable you to run a group for potential small group leaders. We use the word potential advisedly as the idea is that this group of individuals do not have to be committed to become leaders; they can be involved in the training group as a way of seeing if it is something they may want to do in the future. In this way more people are gaining an understanding and indeed experience of small group life which will benefit them and any group that they may be a part of or indeed lead in the future. To help this training be as accessible as possible we have devised it in three sections.

Read:
The first section contains material to be read by each participant on their own prior to joining the training group. This gives biblical background and looks at the beliefs and values that underlie small groups. This is further complimented with looking at how small groups sit within the broader picture of church life and the connections made between them and other church activities. This reading lays the foundations for an understanding of small groups and has reflection questions within it to help the trainees apply it to their particular situation.

Discuss:
The second section contains material for discussion. So it is at this point that the training group meets together. This section has three parts designed to be discussed across three sessions, we suggest each session runs for around 90 mins making it practical to run in an evening. The material for each of these discussion

meetings is read beforehand by the participants. The group facilitator can give a brief overview of the different sections and lead the discussion around the questions at the end of each section. We have also included a welcome question to ask at the beginning of each session which we anticipate will be answered by each person in turn to set the atmosphere to be one of participation and discussion.

Experience:
The third section contains three outlines for the group to experience. We use a simple and well tested format to create an experience of small group life which demonstrates how the previous two sections can be worked out in practice. The idea is that this last section gives a taste of how a small group can run and be effective, demonstrating facilitative leadership, participation and learning shared from the group through this experience!

So it works like this
You read the opening three chapters on your own, meet as a group for discussion for three sessions using the next three chapters and then meet for three sessions to see how it works using the outlines and material in the last three chapters, what could be simpler?

Our aim here is to create a viable way to train and equip people to lead small groups making it possible to have more groups in the life of the local church which is often stifled through lack of potential leaders.

Chapter 1
Beliefs

To understand what a small group could look like in terms of the atmospheres created and the things that could happen in the group we need to take a big step away. By doing this we actually look at a much wider picture and ask ourselves 'What is God's dream for us as believers - what are his hopes and aspirations for us?' Then the small group becomes a vehicle for this dream, just like church on a Sunday. It becomes a part of the process by which God's dreams for us and others are worked out. So how do we know what God's dream is? Well of course we find it in scripture and there are a few places in scripture where it seems to be given to us in a very concise format. One of these is found in Mark 12:28-29, where Jesus is asked:

> *"Of all the commandments, which is the most important?" "The most important one," answered Jesus, "is this: 'Hear, O Israel: The Lord our God, the Lord is one. Love the Lord your God with all your heart and with all your soul and with all your mind and with all your strength.' The second is this: 'Love your neighbour as yourself.' There is no commandment greater than these."*

We can see four places where our love should be focused from these verses.

Firstly, in this passage of scripture we have a hint of God's dream, the Lord our God is one. God wants us to know what he is like and that in heaven is a God of love and relationship. He is good and he wants us all to understand that and to have an opportunity to love him with all our heart and minds and strength.

This speaks of relationship, of friendship. This speaks of God being with us in the hard times when life is really difficult, and it speaks of God being with us in the good times. So church in whatever shape it is found, is here to help us on this spiritual journey and to grow us in our relationship with God. Our small group plays a vital part in this as we will see later.

Secondly, it is not just a place where the focus is on us as individuals and our relationship with God. This dream is more than us just loving God, it is God's dream that we might love one another, that we would have an opportunity as Christians to build community. In doing this we show what God is like as he himself lives in a community of relationships as Father, Son and Holy Spirit. Jesus said, 'By the love that you have for one another they will know that you are my disciples'. In other words when we listen to one another, when we encourage, when we take care of practical needs we are fulfilling God's dream, we are demonstrating real love and it is our belief that a great place for this to happen is in small groups where relationships can be built.

Thirdly, we are also to love ourselves. It is God's dream that each one of us would be whole. Sadly, however strong we are, we all carry some kind of collateral damage from life itself. When this commandment says that we are to love ourselves it is speaking of God's dream of wholeness and healing and that as we participate in church we should be healed and restored as individuals.

Fourthly, there is another focus of our love here. When it says love our neighbour it is not just thinking of our fellow Christians but it is thinking of God's wider world. It is God's dream that every Christian could in their own way, through their gifts and their lives, bring a little bit more love, and care into our world and that our lives can make a difference. It is our belief that this is what church should do and this is what small groups should do as part of the church – they empower you to love others.

So our beliefs encompass something of God's dream but our beliefs also encompass church, this extraordinary organisation that God created - his body. We might want to reflect on what we believe about church and to do this we want to look at scripture, the glimpses that we can see in the New Testament and the early church. We also want to look at some examples from church history and this will give us some understanding of what should be happening in church today. So from the dream we could perhaps draw three strands of DNA that are at the heart of church life and are expressed through the lives of each believer.

Strand 1	We know that God loves us and we want to know and follow him.
Strand 2	We love one another and we build caring Christian community.
Strand 3	We love a lost world and each one of us seeks to make a difference.

Behind these three strands of DNA is an important implicit understanding which is that this commandment was given by Jesus for everyone, that we are all called to do these things. It is not just leaders, it is you and I that are called to love God, to build community and to love a lost world.

So what is the nature of church, what are our beliefs around it? Well, the New Testament is not a manual or a text book but it does give us snippets and pictures. When we see the early church begin to gather in the book of Acts we see them in two places. In Acts 2:46 they are attending the Temple daily where they listen to teaching and they worship together:

> *'Every day they continued to meet together in the temple courts. They broke bread in their homes and ate together with glad and sincere hearts,'*

In this verse we begin to get a picture of the early church, meeting in the temple which is a big space and where they will have had teaching and inspiration and a certain amount of leadership. They then met in their homes which would have been about community and the outworking of their faith. This is their equivalent of our Sunday morning meeting. Secondly, they met in their homes where they break bread and have fellowship together, so church is operating in these two spheres.

Also in the book of Acts we get other pictures of the life of the early church as found in 1 Corinthians 14-26:

> *'When you come together, each of you has a hymn, or a word of instruction, a revelation, a tongue or an interpretation. Everything must be done so that the church may be built up'*

Whenever we see 'each of you' or the 'each ones' in the New Testament we ask ourselves 'what is the context?' Which of the two spheres is this operating in? Obviously this particular verse is not talking about a big meeting and, as we all know from Sunday church this is a wonderful place, but it is not a place of personal contribution. A small group is: in a small group I can share my thoughts, my ideas and my hymn.

In the New Testament there is another phrase, 'one another', this phrase comes up over 130 times. Galatians 6:2 *'Carry each other's burdens'*. Ephesians 4:2 *'...bearing with one another in love'*. Ephesians 4:32 *'Be kind and compassionate to one another, forgiving each other'*. Ephesians 5:19 *'...speaking to one another with psalms, hymns and songs..'.* and on it goes. We need to think about where these 'one anothers' are going to take place? Some could happen on a Sunday morning but most of them are going to happen either on a one to one basis or in the context of our small group. This becomes a natural environment for us to encourage one another.

So we see how important it is to have a context for the 'each ones' and the 'one anothers' and as we seek to understand the early church we realise that their small groups were the foundation of church. They met in the large group for worship, teaching and encouragement as and when it was possible, due to persecution or other factors. So in the first 300 years of the church the small group would have been the most important component of church. However, as church became legal and was adopted by the Roman Empire we see the buildings and the Sunday worship becoming more and more important. At first held in a balance and then later with small groups disappearing and church on a Sunday becoming the strongest component part.

Throughout church history we see these two structures and for most of this time the structure of the big meeting has taken over and that has become synonymous with how we understand church. There is nothing wrong with this but over time many have argued that there are some things that are lost when the smaller meeting does not play as equal and important part as the larger gathering.

If we look at this in more detail we can see that both the bigger meeting and the smaller meeting have strengths. There is something special about worshipping in a large gathering, about being in an environment to hear good teaching. Christians have met on a Sunday for thousands of years and experienced these good things. But there are also things that cannot happen on a Sunday. When we think of real community, of really knowing people's needs, this is hard to make happen on a Sunday. When we think of our own participation and what to bring as an individual in the context of the 'one anothers' or 'each ones', this becomes the strength of a small group. The 'one anothers' also imply an accountability, a sense that someone else knows who we are and they encourage us in our walk of faith. If we are thinking of, say, the energy for mission, we all know that someone can stand up on a Sunday and ask us to do this or that but it is very hard to have any real accountability to that type of call. However, this can be worked out very practically in a small group that has adopted loving a lost world as an important focus. Here, making a difference where you live and where you work is important, so we can encourage one another to see this challenge happen and to follow it through. This is because of the strength of the relationships that can come in a small group context.

So our belief is that church works best when it expresses itself in the big and the small. Bill Beckham expressed this as a two winged church linking it to the idea of a bird that can soar and fly. If there is just one wing operating i.e. just the big groupwing, then the bird will not be able to fly as it was originally designed to do, both wings need to be operating together. History also tells us this is important. Joel Comisky, who has written extensively around church life and small groups in his book *'2000 Years of Small Groups'* shows us how again and again the church realises that just meeting on a Sunday is not enough and this fantastic book gives us a picture of the difference small groups have made to church life down through the centuries.

In the United Kingdom we have our own great illustration of the wonder of small groups. If we go back to the 1730s and look at the church then we see some interesting things. The basic message of church was 'come' and it was all about that Sunday meeting. Most of the ministry and activity of the church was done by the leaders; the church members were mainly passive and the influence of church on the wider society was quite small and its most obvious expression was the Sunday meeting.

Into this stepped a man named John Wesley, an Anglican clergyman who had an encounter with God that so challenged and changed him that he dared to go back to first principles and ask himself questions about the shape, the nature, and the structure of church. He read his New Testament and began to get ideas by seeing what happened in the early church. He met a radical group from Germany called the Moravians and they had all sorts of new ideas and structures. Then, through his meetings in London and Bristol, as people began to hear his message and come to faith, he began an experiment of organising church in two different contexts. He believed all his life in the importance of Sunday and the place of worship, preaching and teaching in this context but he realised that if he was going to fulfil God's dream, as we described earlier, he needed something else. So he created small groups which became known as classes.

For John Wesley church began to change, no longer was the emphasis on 'come' but the emphasis was on 'go' - let's make a difference, let's change the world, let's take this Christian message to every sphere of society to make an impact where we live and where we work. The leaders stopped doing all the work and began to encourage others to do it, the church members became disciples and were active in their faith and the influence got bigger and bigger and bigger.

This new kind of church was held together by the power of the class system as it became known, which was the 'building block' of church life. In your class meeting if you were walking with God you were given your ticket which enabled you to go to church on a Sunday. This church began to grow and over the next 100 years, both through Methodism and through other forms of church at that time, there was a huge spiritual awakening. We believe that church in the small, through the class system of John Wesley, had a major part to play in this awakening.

For reflection

How would you describe the DNA of your church?

Chapter 2
Values

In this chapter Laurence encourages us to think about how our beliefs shape our values and our values then shape our actions and behaviour. It is, therefore, important when joining a group to understand the values that might be drawn from the beliefs already described in Chapter 1. Phil Potter, in his excellent book *'The Challenge of Cell Church'* lays out five values which many groups and churches have embraced. The strength of this particular idea is that, even if the groups across the church meet at different times, in different places and perhaps embrace different formats, there is a similarity if they have all adopted the same values. Phil uses a simple device of A B C D E to describe these values and here is a synopsis of them.

A is for: All Involved

As we saw earlier in Mark 12:29 Jesus says the following in response to a question about which is the greatest commandment:

> *'The most important one,'* answered Jesus, *'is this: "Hear, O Israel: the Lord our God, the Lord is one. Love the Lord your God with all your heart and with all your soul and with all your mind, and with all your strength." The second is this: "Love your neighbour as yourself." There is no commandment greater than these.'*

When Jesus spoke these immortal words he was addressing his disciples and he was addressing us. The implication of this passage is that these commands are for all of us. It is not just special people who love God and do the right thing, God wants us all to be involved.

Over the last 30 years the body of Christ in the UK has gone through a number of changes, paradigm shifts if you like, and one of the most powerful ones is that we have gone from a church that is all about leaders and a few special people to a church that is increasingly about us all. We have recognised that, for the body of Christ to make a difference in this country, for us to grow, then leader power alone will not achieve this. It is through the participation of every member of the body of Christ that we all learn to be the people that God wants us to be and each one of us can make our own special contribution.

Now, in some ways this is such a simple and common sense idea that you would expect it to be happening everywhere. However, in many churches 80% of the work is still done by 20% of the people and overcoming centuries of influence where the body of Christ has been passive rather than active takes time. Also, there are other internal factors that often hold us back. It would appear that many of us suffer from what we can call a negative self-image or a negative script. So when it comes to doing things in the life of our church we hear an all too familiar voice in our heads that says – not you, remember your last failure, you can't do this – and we are held back from doing what God might want us to do. It could equally be the influence of our education, our background, our past experience, that robs us of getting involved: our fears and anxieties.

My experience over many years is that if we embrace the value of everyone involved our small group gives us the perfect place in a safe environment for our faith to grow from passive to active. For us to begin to hear the sound of our own voice, a place where we can pray, a place where we can contribute, this can be truly life changing. I have recently seen a couple join a small group who came from a background where they were not expected to participate. They had not prayed out loud, they had not shared their thoughts, they perhaps had not seen how their lives could influence others and yet through the small group they have become involved and it is a delight to see their participation and growth.

B is for: Becoming Disciples

Matthew 5:1-2 'His disciples came to him, and he began to teach them.'

We know from this verse and many others that we are all called to be disciples, to be followers and we can understand why this might be important, that we are, as scripture says, 'not just hearers, but doers of the word.' That as much as possible we are seeking to put our Christianity into practice and this is important for all sorts of reasons. It is our worship to God, but it is also, in our post-modern and sceptical world, our most powerful witness. We live at a moment in history where, as a culture, we have become cynical about words. We are no longer prepared to trust words as we have seen too many instances of important people saying one thing and doing something quite different. It is interesting that when the disciples of John came to Jesus and they asked 'Are you the one?' he didn't give them a bible study, he said to them tell John what you see, what you experience. The life of Jesus, his witness, his discipleship, spoke volumes.

So, in a small group we will all be on a journey, a pathway of discipleship and this perhaps will have some characteristics to it. This could be one of the very first places where we have the courage to be honest and ask for prayer because at times we all find the Christian life difficult. This could be a place of honesty for us, this could be a place where we do not just hear scripture but we wrestle together to understand how that might work in our complex lives of today's culture. It is also a place, because we are on this journey with others, where we can experience the encouragement and the sense of togetherness. Holding each other accountable is a powerful experience in helping us to grow, to change, and to live out the Christian life. As Bill Beckham so helpfully puts it 'being responsible to and for one another.'

C is for: Creating Community

John 13:35 'By this everyone will know that you are my disciples, if you love one another.'

In this powerful statement Jesus is telling us about the power of community, that if we as Christians are connected together in a genuine way this is not just of benefit to us but it is a demonstration to the world of the reality of the Christian message. It is true to say that when we go to church on a Sunday there is a measure of community and that is a good thing but when we are in a small group we can step into a whole new level of community. What does this look like? For example, in our group we had a lady suffering from chronic fatigue syndrome which meant for a number of years she had no energy whatsoever and so for the small group this was an opportunity for the community to cook meals and to help support a family in crisis. At other times it is just simple things; a word, a phone call, a cup of coffee, those human connections that in some way carry the spirit of the divine God who himself lives in community as Father, Son and Holy Spirit. As we all grow in community and learn to give and receive what is the currency of the Kingdom of God, we not only benefit in the now but we become community carriers and we take this simple idea of community into our wider world. In a sense we become carriers of the kingdom of God as we do this.

In talking to a senior policeman responsible for a good sized town here in England, he said that 40% of the work his officers do relates to the breakdown of community. Nothing to do with policing in the real sense of the word, they were responding to calls of loneliness, responding to things that a good neighbour could do. So as we learn community in our small group we take community wherever we go and it is transformational.

A young woman worked in an office building that was really quite cold in terms of its atmosphere and nobody knew one another; it wasn't a great place to be. But this young woman, an ordinary church member who had experienced community in her small group, brought its essence into this workplace. Her warm smile, her conversations, her getting to know everybody, joining the threads together began to bring a warmth that thawed the cold atmosphere. It restored a sense of community that this particular space had not seen for a very long time. So in your small group you will experience community and you will become part of community as you give and receive and care together.

D is for: Doing Evangelism

Matthew 5:13 'You are the salt of the earth' 5:14 'You are the light of the world.'

In these two little phrases Jesus is speaking to us about our evangelism, about our mission. In Matthew 28:28 the disciples are told to go. There is probably no greater challenge that we face as Christians than the sharing of our faith and making a difference where we work and where we live. The word evangelism is the stuff of nightmares for many; pictures of standing on soap boxes float before the eyes, knocking on doors, speaking when no one wants to listen. It's terrifying and so the challenge is to understand what being missional is, what doing evangelism is in today's culture. And how we can live out our faith and share our faith in ways that are appropriate, dynamic, doable and not terrifying! It is my experience that this value is one of the hardest to take root in the life of a small group and in the life of church as a whole. We know we should be doing mission but we are not quite sure what this is and so the reality is we don't do very much.

In our small group we have an opportunity to learn together, to go on a journey of discovery amongst friends, and as we do this we find that mission begins in the heart. It starts as a question; do we care about people? John 3:16 tells us that *'God so loved the world'*, his motivation is love and that is why he sends his Son. So we can pray that God will give us big hearts and we can realise astonishing things. For example, in a recent survey by Barna Group called Talking Jesus *(www.talkingjesus.org)* we learn that over 60% of people who come to faith are members of our family or our friends therefore in the simplest terms doing evangelism is about being a good family member. It is about having unchurched friends, being acquainted with people and connected with people who don't go to church. As you do life in a natural way with them, living out your Christian values, telling your story where appropriate, inviting them to carol services, Easter services, suddenly doing evangelism becomes an easier thing. We can all be a better family member!

We have seen churches over the last 10 years or so stepping out into social action, through food banks, street pastors, giving money advice, and so many other initiatives. Doing evangelism is also about being a volunteer in these initiatives, helping in the food bank, the mums and toddler project. Through these volunteering connections we share our faith.

So the role of the small group is to spend a few moments each week praying for the relationships we have, we pray for one another to keep on reaching out, to be involved in the projects that our church might be doing, inviting people where appropriate to church events. My experience is that to stay missional, to keep on reaching out, takes energy and encouragement and we can receive a measure of that in our big meetings on a Sunday. However, if we make this value a part of our small group it empowers us on an ongoing basis in the specific areas that are relevant to us as individuals.

E is for: Encountering God

> *Luke 19:5-8. 'When Jesus reached the spot, he looked up and said to him, "Zacchaeus, come down immediately. I must stay at your house today." So he came down at once and welcomed him gladly. All the people saw this and began to mutter, "He has gone to be the guest of a sinner." But Zacchaeus stood up and said to the Lord, "Look, Lord! Here and now I give half of my possessions to the poor, and if I have cheated anybody out of anything, I will pay back four times the amount."'*

In these amazing verses we read the story of Zacchaeus encountering Jesus and its transformational effect and perhaps one of the most clearly understood purposes of small groups is to encounter God. Yes this happens as we meet on a Sunday but there is something very personal and life changing about meeting God in a small group. This happens through our grappling with scripture together, through our honesty and vulnerability and being prayed for, through the joy of praying for others, in learning to give and receive. Suddenly it is as if God has stepped out of the shadows and into a much more intimate and close space with us and the intensity of our faith and our experience goes up a jot or two; something special is taking place.

Many small groups around the country have a time of worship that is not necessarily singing as this can be hard in a small group. We might instead reflect on scripture, on creation, listen to music and through these different experiences we encounter God.

Asking who wants prayer is a vital part of the life of a small group and in this context it is not such a big step to say, 'pray for me, I am going through a hard time, my situation is difficult.' As we are prayed for we encounter the living God. Alternatively, as we pray for someone else, we encounter God through seeing our prayer make a difference. Small groups become that safe place where we can experiment, experience and encounter God in all sorts of different ways.

Values into practice

The following shows how the values we have just looked at are outworked in your small group. It shows something of what the meeting will look like as these values are applied. It also highlights some of the dynamics around leadership that help the values to be a reality in the group.

All Involved:

Small group dynamics. Welcome is key to making sure everyone's voice is heard in each meeting. Everyone contributes something. The work of hospitality and leading is shared. New as well as established Christians are involved in leading.

Leadership dynamics. I seek to identify the gifts of other cell members and help them to use them. I encourage the leadership of others. I facilitate others to lead the group meetings and seek not to be leading more than one section of the meeting myself.

Becoming Disciples:

Small group dynamics. Members are seeking to grow closer to God. And to live out their faith actively. They seek to be accountable to each other. The word section of the meeting is not merely discussion, but involves prayer for each other as we apply what we have learned to our lives.

Leadership dynamics. I develop my own relationship with God and seek to allow the Holy Spirit to work in every area of my life. I am open and accountable to others in my walk with God. I encourage the group to apply the bible's teaching and values practically to their lives.

Creating Community:

Small group dynamics. Hospitality is warm towards each and every person. Community grows by prayer, care and sharing in a small group. People feel safe with each other and share deeply. People show care for each other outside the meeting. Others as well as the leader help to facilitate community.

Leadership dynamics. I have a pastor's heart for each member of the group and love them sacrificially. I facilitate the quality of care for each other inside and outside the meeting. My personal openness creates the environment for other people's real problems to surface and be dealt with.

Doing Evangelism:

Small group dynamics. The group longs to see more people discover Jesus and has a growing vision for sharing God's love outside the church. The group prays for people who do not yet know Jesus. The group works together to regularly reach out beyond church boundaries e.g. social events, practical service, running Alpha.

Leadership dynamics. My personal commitment to pray for one to three friends. I place a high priority on helping the group to work together to share God's love – making sure we are always engaged in or working towards the next opportunity to reach out.

Encountering God:

Small group dynamics. A sense of God's presence when the group meets. Time given to worship and prayer. Encountering God changes people's lives. We hear and discuss God's word.

Leadership dynamics. My personal relationship with God. My expectation that he changes people's lives. I make sure quality time is given to worship and this is led in a way that enables those there to engage. I make sure the bible is applied to our lives and space is given for us to respond to its challenges.

For reflection

Which of the values listed here would you say is the strongest in your church?

Why do you think this is?

Which of the values would you say is the weakest?

Why do you think this is?

Chapter 3
Where do small groups fit?

It is our belief that small groups play a vital part in church life, they are the building blocks and have a place at the very heart of the church. However, they are often seen as just one of the many programs run by the church. Thinking of them in this way does not give them the centrality and profile that they need to thrive and become the beating heart that enlivens and gives energy to the body of the church as a whole.

A helpful way to think about their place in the life of any church is to consider them structurally like a wing of the church. This is sometimes called the community wing as this is one of the primary functions of these small groups because they are places where relationships are built and community is experienced. The second wing is the larger group gathering and associated church structures. These two wings need to work together and be connected to each other just as they are in a bird and as they work together they enable a sense of flight. Often the church leadership attention is only given to one wing, the larger gathering and other church structures. This creates an inbalance and the connections to the small group wing can be overlooked. So let's see how these connections might be made and what it will take to keep the connections healthy and vibrant.

It is important that church leadership and church members have some idea of how the small groups and the bigger dynamics of church work in partnership together. So if we think for a moment about the aspects of the big group wing of the church there are five dynamics that we could think of: teaching, church life, mission, leadership and pastoral care.

So the central leaders of the church take some responsibility for the big picture, the legal frameworks, the pastoral care, the meetings on Sunday and the support of small groups. They also oversee the missional direction of the church, and the empowering of the members of the church into their calling in the whole of life.

The place of the small group is to provide a different context where there is a degree of leadership. There is the facilitation of members to minister to one another, to apply what is taught on a Sunday, to encourage one another in discipleship and reaching out in a missional context through their friendships, their workplace. As Mark Greene from LICC describes it: their frontline. Many churches running good small groups encourage their groups to work with the teaching given on Sundays. Their task here is to help those in the group apply the message to their lives and help each other work out how they can follow Jesus in everyday life. We will look at this in greater detail in the following chapter.

So how does this partnership work? Obviously the big group wing of church is giving space for the small groups to exist and is involved in the training and selecting of leaders to run these groups and providing the ongoing support and training these leaders might need. It is true to say that, in our experience, whenever small groups decline in terms of their effectiveness it is often due to the fact that the support structure for the small group leaders has not been effective enough.

Partnership between the big group wing and small group wing

Church in the big and the small has been a strand in church history from the early history of the church through to today. We have the wonderful example of Methodism and John Wesley's passion for church to work at both these levels. He visited small groups which he called classes throughout his life in ministry. He reports that on Thursday 17 July 1760 he visited a small group in Limerick. He was concerned that their classes were not delivering spiritual life, zeal and activity. At other times, he was concerned about preaching, communion and the big picture. We know that this dynamic partnership of church in the big and the small changed this nation as people were empowered to live for Jesus in every area of their lives.

Churches in the UK who have worked with the small group idea have worked best when they have understood this partnership and kept these two areas in balance. Church in the big supplies the overall leadership and framework, not only making sure that Sunday church works, but that the pastoral structure of the church is in place and its missional purpose and small group leaders are properly resourced.

The Group Coach

We have learnt that for church in the big to really know what is happening in the small groups, someone needs to visit them. This small group coach needs to be somebody who understands the DNA, can visit a small group and assess whether this group is working and flourishing. The important thing is to know what is actually happening in the groups and the best way to ascertain this is by visiting them. You can pick up a certain amount by talking to the leader of the group, but they inevitably see what is happening in the group through their own filters. For this reason it is good to have someone from the outside going in who can bring a more objective view. This also communicates a sense of value to the leader and the group as a whole. The fact that time is being given and support offered to the leader and the group speaks volumes about the value of the group in the life of the church at large.

The other crucial role we have seen these group coaches play is that of being a referral point for those who need more support than the group can offer. We will look at this more later. For some this needs to be ongoing support, for others it is for a short period of time to enable them to cope with the circumstances of life. Many small group leaders become overwhelmed with the needs of some individuals in a group and need someone who can step in to help. This is the role of the coach. They can offer a variety of help either from within the church or sometimes by professional bodies outside the church. This means that the individuals who need support do not see the small group as the solution to all their problems and avoid sucking the life out of it and the leader. We will look at this in more detail and open it up for discussion in Chapter 6.

Supporting the leaders

Another part of big wing support of the small groups is how the leaders of the groups are valued and developed. Many churches in the UK have taken this on board and given it attention and priority. We have seen leaders gathered together for feedback and prayer. This happens every eight to ten weeks, sometimes over breakfast on a Saturday morning. Time is spent sharing what has been going on in the groups and cross fertilising good practice and ideas. This strengthens the feeling of team amongst the small group leaders. It is a good opportunity to pray for each other and have a renewed sense of commitment together to see the groups and individuals in them encouraged and growing.

A good number of churches have developed a pattern of ongoing development of their leaders by running a day away each year with specific training and greater time to share and pray for each other. In some cases this has been a weekend away where the team dynamic is further strengthened and increased time is available to resource and support these leaders in their front line role. As you can imagine this sends a very strong message to the rest of the church about how important these groups are in the life of the church when this amount of time and energy is put into their support and wellbeing.

All these things often go unnoticed but are essential to keep the small groups healthy and ensure their ongoing development. Many small group leaders fail, burn out or simply give up because they feel undervalued and unsupported.

A vision for mission

Another role that the big wing offers is that of casting and keeping a vision for mission. For example, one large church in England with holistic small groups puts focus on the missional dynamic of 'loving your neighbour' at least four times a year. They know that this is important and groups need that continual encouragement. In the same way they emphasise why church is best in the big and the small. Sustaining this way of being church over many years means keeping the ideas alive and enthusing new members along the way. The key factors of church life, the key factors of walking in the Christian way, need to be repeated on an ongoing basis.

Communication

The two-way flow of communication between central church leaders and small group leaders is vital in this dynamic partnership. It leads to well supported small groups and relevant initiatives for the whole church in outreach and training.

So in a number of ways we start to see how the two wings of the church are connected together and the increased dynamic and energy that this brings.

We can see how these two structures help one another. Each is important but there does need to be a real commitment to the idea of the two wings. Without a strong conviction that small groups are vital the Sunday dynamic of church can easily take over. We have seen many churches lose their focus on small groups and they decline or cease altogether. When this happens then much is lost in terms of real community, the participation of people and the opportunity to mobilise the local church in mission and effective church life.

For reflection

How are the small groups in your church linked to the larger life of the church?

Chapter 4
Using the bible in our small groups

One of the areas that the 'one another' statements of the New Testament can be outworked is in our small groups. There are fifty eight of them in total and we will not list them all here, but a couple come to mind when we think about how we use our bibles in a small group setting.

> *'Let the message of Christ dwell among you richly as you teach and admonish one another with all wisdom through psalms, hymns, and songs from the Spirit, singing to God with gratitude in your hearts.'* Colossians 3:16

> *'Therefore encourage one another and build each other up, just as in fact you are doing.'* 1 Thessalonians 5:11

Leading the bible study part of a small group can seem like an overwhelming task that needs expert biblical knowledge, a degree in teaching and group interaction. So let's shed a few myths about this before we look at how to lead this section.

What you are **not** doing:

You are **not** leading a bible study
You are **not** teaching as if in a classroom
You are **not** showing off your expertise on a subject
You are **not** re-teaching the sermon from Sunday
You are **not** leading a discussion group

So what am I doing you may well ask, is there anything left?

Well yes you are leading people from the theoretical understanding of a message or scripture, to practical application, usually through a time of ministry. This will often be based out of what was preached on Sunday and is about the application of this to the lives of the individuals in the group, as in James 1:22-25:

> *'Do not merely listen to the word, and so deceive yourselves. Do what it says. Anyone who listens to the word but does not do what it says is like someone who looks at his face in a mirror and, after looking at himself, goes away and immediately forgets what he looks like. But whoever looks intently into the perfect law that gives freedom, and continues in it - not forgetting what they have heard, but doing it - they will be blessed in what they do'.*

There are several stages that we can consider to help us achieve this and to act as an outline for us to use in the group. These stages are best expressed as follows:

Stage 1   What is God saying?
Stage 2   Connecting with experience
Stage 3   Ministry time

Let's look at each one in turn.

Stage 1 - What is God saying?

As Christians we believe in a God who reveals himself to us, and his primary vehicle for this is his word given to us through scripture. We should therefore have an anticipation that God will speak as we engage with scripture together in our group.

So we start by reviewing what was in the message from Sunday and read the main passage of scripture that was used. This of course assumes that most of us heard the message or have listened online in the meantime.

If that is not the case then whoever is leading may need to do a short résumé of the main points.

Then ask:

What seems to be the main point of this passage or what does this passage say to us today?

You need to give time for people to respond and you may want to ask the same question again in a slightly different way if a response is slow in coming.

Then ask:

What stands out to you in this passage?

It is important that you acknowledge people's answers with a thank you or head nod. As one person finishes look around expectantly for the next contribution. Again, give time and encourage responses. Keep a mental note of key points so you can summarise.

These first two questions get us connecting with the scripture itself and what the preacher brought on Sunday. We now want to move to the application of what has come up. If questions are raised it is helpful to refer them back to the group as a whole rather than necessarily trying to answer them yourself.

It is good to summarise at this point and draw together a common truth from what has been shared. You will probably have an idea of what this might be as you will have spent time preparing beforehand, but go with what God is highlighting in the group rather than bringing your pre-formed answers.

Stage 2 - Connecting with experience

To move to application, ask:

How can you illustrate this truth from an experience in your own life?

This draws people in and helps them see how a particular truth can be lived out in practice. You may need to ask clarifying questions as people share. If something is not clear to you it probably isn't clear to the rest of the group. You may have to start things moving here with an illustration from your own life, but don't be too quick to jump in as you want to encourage participation by the group.

As stories are shared, a sense of reality is created and we begin to see how God has grown us and applied his truth to our lives in the past. This takes what we have been doing from a theoretical idea and fleshes it out in practice. This builds a very real sense of community and as we share our experiences together we get an insight into each other's lives and how we have related to God and seen him at work.

Stage 3 - Ministry time

The climax of our word time should be seeing God move among us as he ministers to us through those in the group. Sounds great, doesn't it! But how do we encourage it to happen! This is where the faith dynamic kicks in. We need to ask a question that leads to ministry and allows people to respond to what God has been stirring in them through the last two stages. It needs to be something like:

'What is God saying to you right now?' Or , 'Who needs help?'

If you are not the small group leader it may be that you will need to ask the leader to ask this question for you if you feel it requires more leadership than you are able to bring to the group. If so, then make sure you talk to your group leader beforehand and ask them to do this for you. We would really encourage you to go with this final question and expect God to move through you as you ask it and lead the group to pray and minister to those who respond.

Some tips to encourage a ministry response

Pray, pray, pray!

Pray that God will give you a specific word for someone in the group that will lead to ministry.

Activity aids response. Asking the group to stand as you ask the 'who needs help?' question encourages people to be active spiritually as they are active physically. This also means that you are all on your feet as you start to pray and can gather round an individual where appropriate.

You may also want to move a chair into the centre of the room in anticipation of someone sitting in it and the group gathering around to pray.

Some tips in ministry time

Encourage people to bring scriptures, pictures, prophecy and words of knowledge as you pray together. Even if they themselves cannot see the relevance of what they are sharing, someone else in the group often brings understanding and interpretation. Encourage people to lay hands on the individuals being ministered to appropriately if they are comfortable with that.

Start by praying that God will move through you all as you pray.

Be aware of any response from the person being prayed for and act accordingly, for example are they moved emotionally with tears, and do they need a tissue?

Don't rush things to a conclusion. It is often helpful as the ministry comes to an end to ask if anyone has anything from God that they have not yet shared or prayed out.

In summary

We want to see people edified, as outlined in Ephesians 4:11-16:

> 'So Christ himself gave the apostles, the prophets, the evangelists, the pastors and teachers, to equip his people for works of service, so that the body of Christ may be built up until we all reach unity in the faith and in the knowledge of the Son of God and become mature, attaining to the whole measure of the fullness of Christ. Then we will no longer be infants, tossed back and forth by the waves, and blown here and there by every wind of teaching and by the cunning and craftiness of men in their deceitful scheming. Instead, speaking the truth in love, we will in all things grow up into him who is the head, that is, Christ. From him the whole body, joined and held together by every supporting ligament, grows and builds itself up in love, as each part does its work.'

Our objective is to encourage each other to grow in maturity as we share our lives together and minister to one another as God leads us in response to his word.

We can think of this as a bit like building a house. We start with an idea which is in the form of plans drawn on paper. This is the theory part, we imagine what it can look like and how it will take shape. We then apply these plans and start building from them and see a house come into being. The plans on their own are not much use, you can't live in a set of plans, they need to be used! So it is with the word of God, we need to use it to shape our lives, not just have it as a theoretical idea.

For reflection

What does small group leadership need to look like for the above to happen?

What atmospheres need to be in place in the group for this area to work well?

Something to discuss - an introduction

Having read the opening four chapters on your own the aim of these next three chapters is to get together and discuss the content with others who may be looking to lead a group at some point in the future. This can be done in a number of ways as best suits the group. Our suggestion would be to use the chapters that follow as content that you read prior to getting together and then have a brief reminder of the content as you go through each section in the group. Use the questions at the end of each section to stimulate discussion. So as you read you might want to make a note of your own observations and answers to the questions so you can bring them to the discussion group.

The next three chapters cover the following areas:

- Group dynamics
- Supporting small group leaders
- Small group evangelism - Laurence's reflections

How will these chapters work?

To enable you to get the best out of the material we have divided each week into sections and given some timings beside them so you are able to cover the content effectively. We have assumed that the time you will be together for each session will be around 90 mins. If you have more or less time simply adjust the timings accordingly. Each session (chapter) opens with a welcome question which is designed to give everyone in the group an opportunity to speak and set the tone of the group from the outset as this is designed to be an opportunity for people to contribute rather than just listen to the voice of the leader.

Chapter 5
Group dynamics

Welcome question
What do you most enjoy about being part of a small group?

Section 1 (20 mins)

Participation a key ingredient

The first section here gives us some background to why our small groups are participatory in nature. We will then move on to look at how you as a leader can facilitate the group to enable everyone to make a meaningful contribution.

Jesus painted a different future for his followers. In the Old Testament, we see that the work of God is done by the prophets, priests and kings. We see in the New Testament that the religious people, the Pharisees, the Sadducees and Rabbis, speak for God and do the work of God. Jesus however is creating a whole new model. Our devotion to God is not through an intermediary. We are all to be active carriers of God's love and purpose.

It seems implicit in the descriptions of the spread of the early church that in the first 100 years or so Christianity was carried as a people movement. Its spread across the Roman Empire was not just the work of a few apostles and bishops, but it was individuals, hundreds and thousands of them, doing the work of God, bearing testimony to their Jesus that was so compelling. Yet, sadly, as the church became established within buildings it became organized into different groupings and the Old Testament model crept back in. Church can seem once again to be a place where the priests are the intermediary in worship. They do the work of God and the people become passive followers.

Changes begin to happen once you introduce small groups into the life of a church. In his book *'2000 Years of Small Groups'* Joel Comiskey writes:

'The early church saw itself as God's new family. Their intense familial love permeated the meetings. As brothers and sisters in Christ's new family, they wanted to serve one another as Jesus served his own disciples. This is why the phrase 'one another' appears more than fifty times in the New Testament. These phrases instructed the early believers on how to cultivate relationships among themselves.'

Take away the small groups and slowly but surely the contribution of 'the everyone' ceases. We arrive at the sort of equations that are well known in the church today, that 80% of the work is done by 20% of the people.

What happens in these small groups which intentionally embrace the concept of people power? In essence, these groups are seeking to fulfil the Great Commandment, which is to 'love the Lord your God with all your heart mind and strength and your neighbour as yourself' and the Great Commission: namely 'to go into the world and make disciples' so they encourage both mission and discipleship. In today's language we might say they are both 'connected and authentic.'

These small groups aspire to be a place where authentic wholeness and discipleship are pursued and where being encouraged and equipped to connect with those outside the church is at the heart of the idea. A part of this authentic process is that groups become a place of healing as people are supported, encouraged and prayed for.

To enable both of these things to have a practical outcome rather than just be theoretical ideas a small group needs do something else. It needs to give space and opportunity. In a big meeting, only a few can genuinely make their contribution, and that is how it should be. But in a small meeting, there is an unlimited opportunity, particularly if it is well led, for all to contribute and participate.

Small groups not only give opportunity for us all to contribute but in groups which embrace the fullness of the Great Commission, there is opportunity and encouragement for each person to become active in how they can be part of God's purpose in the world throughout their week, where they live and where they work.

One aspect that enables this is to do with the size of the group.

What size of group are we talking about? In looking at the experience here in the UK, the best practice that we have seen over these last years, is that groups work best at a number somewhere between four and twelve. Four is nearly too few and twelve is nearly too many. Once you have twelve in a room, the capacity for participation is significantly reduced.

Why is this? It's to do with the number of lines of communication between the people in the group. Where you have three people in a group you have six lines of communication two between persons

A and B two between persons B and C and two between C and A. This makes the group feel quite intimate and gives plenty of opportunity for participation. The way that the number of lines of communication can be worked out is to simply apply a little formula, which is taking the number of people in the group and multiplying it by the number in the group, then taking away the number in the group so with our example of three it would mean 3 x 3 = 9 – 3 = 6. And if you have ten people in your group you have 10 x 10 = 100 – 10 which is 90 lines of communication! Not surprisingly this limits the amount of participation that is possible! We have noticed that it can also limit the attendance of members as the group becomes too large. People don't participate as much and as a result don't feel as connected, so don't come. They also feel that they won't be missed. Many groups can have a list of members, some up to fifteen or more, but in reality only have eight to ten or so in regular attendance.

Questions for discussion

What have you been reminded of or what has struck you for the first time in this opening section?

What do you think about the numbers example shared above?

What is your view about participation and what kind of leadership is required to help this?

Section 2 (20 mins)

Growing yourself and others through participation and leadership

Creating Atmospheres of Growth

One of our challenges as leaders is to create atmospheres of growth. To create environments where people find it easy to 'have a go', to step out, and as a result be better equipped to discover and use their core gifts that have so often been buried or under-utilised through life.

So what creates these environments?

Many of us who are already leaders have travelled quite a distance in our own development but seldom take the opportunity to share in an open and vulnerable way what that has been like for us. So, as with many things, it starts with us sharing our experiences of growth honestly, including the ups and downs.

A culture of experimentation

Many people in our churches believe that they can't 'have a go' at something until they have got everything sorted. As leaders we are also used to hearing "I won't be able to help someone else until I have got my act together completely". Our theology sometimes does not help us here as we often view failure as sin because for so many the Christian life is about 'getting it right'. Trevor is regularly challenged by the words 'go and lo I am with you' from Matthew 28 - it's as we step out that we experience God with us. It's a well known fact that we seldom get things right the first time so we need to create opportunities for having a go. Small groups are of course great incubators for people in this respect.

A need for encouragement

We are constantly amazed at what a little positive encouragement can do. When did you last enable someone to step out of their comfort zone and try something new? It needs to be a regular part of our leadership rhythm to build people up through words of encouragement. A word of warning here in that it is essential to be genuine and specific, otherwise we come across as bland and insincere, giving away praise lightly.

Always looking for potential

Try playing a little scenario game. Every time you meet someone look for their untapped potential, what is it that God sees in them that is being overlooked? Some clues are to see what they get passionate or excited about; what brings them alive that is not yet being outworked in their life. What is in the embryonic stage of development that just needs fanning into flame?

Sorting the issues

For many there are good reasons why they don't want to step out and grow. Are we prepared to put the work in to build relationships and discover some of the obstacles to growth? Sometimes previous hurts and failures have not been dealt with well and we need to walk people through a healing process so they are willing to have another go.

Creating space for people

This is where small groups really come into their own. Trevor recalls the following: 'Recently in the group I attend I was down to lead the welcome and asked "what new skill would you like to learn?" The answers were varied and in some cases quite surprising but even by verbalising them this just created the possibility that they could happen. I even went on e-Bay to try for a woodworking lathe for one of the group (sadly I was outbid) but wouldn't it have been fun to have arrived at the group next week with a surprise present!'

Questions for discussion

Divide the group into pairs and ask them to discuss together:

What has helped you grow as a Christian?

Section 3 (20 mins)

Encouraging participation

An effective way to encourage participation is to create safety at the beginning of the meeting by outlining what has been planned. Share your expectation for the meeting. Explain the type of contribution you are looking for at each section. Clarify any contribution that is made in an unclear fashion.

Repetition: repetition is often helpful and brings clarity

Restating a contribution helps in the following ways:

- Gives it your seal of approval.
- Allows you to confirm that you understood it e.g. "So what you're saying is . . .".
- Allows you to interpret it and vary the language to make it accessible to others.
- Restating a series of contributions allows you to summarise and bring a focus.

Body language

Be aware of the signals you give out by your physical response or posture. Some clues:

- Folded arms says "Don't come close".
- Slouching in the chair communicates "I'm not interested".
- Looking down after you ask a question gives permission for people to answer.
- Eye contact encourages response.
- Nodding encourages people to continue.
- Turning away stops the person who is contributing.

Use good questions

- Learn how to ask related questions to increase understanding.
- Avoid questions that are closed, (i.e. give yes or no answers) and use "what", "when", "how" and "why" questions.

Tips to help you facilitate well and create shared ownership

- Talk in 'we' and 'our' terms about the group and not 'my'. We can often slip into the use of the 'my' language without realising.
- Give away parts of your small group meeting, such as the welcome or worship, which allows others to participate and therefore own the meeting.
- Don't allow yourself to become the answer to everyone's problems but ensure that pastoral care is a corporate issue and so encourage ownership and shared responsibility.
- Get to know your group members well enough to know their strengths and gifts.
- Work towards each person making their contribution out of these strengths (including you).
- Recognise that some people will need help in making their contribution.
- Use phrases such as "that's great, thank you for sharing that". Simply nodding in agreement as someone contributes encourages them to continue. If people feel affirmed they will contribute.
- Try to avoid publicly contradicting someone. A response of "That's very interesting. I would like to talk about that a little more with you sometime", can help. On some occasions you might need to correct heresy but be gentle and loving.

Questions for discussion

How could the atmospheres of growth at the beginning of this section be seen in action?

Ask the group which of the above tips to help you facilitate well, they found most helpful and why?

Section 4 (20 mins)

Helping different people make a healthy contribution to the group

The following are guidelines and advice on how to facilitate different people making their contribution to the group.

The over-talkative person

- Use small group work with time limits, i.e. split into pairs or threes.
- Gently but firmly cut them short if they begin to ramble or dominate. Speak to them privately if necessary.
- Encourage the whole cell to allow one another to participate.
- Pray for the person as you prepare for the cell meeting.

The withdrawn person

- Build a good relationship with the person outside the cell meeting.
- Encourage them during the welcome/refreshment time.
- Draw them out by asking for their opinions (open-ended questions prevent monosyllabic answers).
- Pray for them.
- Ask them to share something specific ahead of the meeting so they have time to think about it.

The argumentative person

- Don't allow the meeting to become a heated debate.
- Deal with sensitive issues privately, one-to-one.
- A persistently argumentative person needs to be confronted, first privately then with another.

- Love the person through the difficulty.
- Pray for them.

The casual attendee

- Draw the person in by involving them somehow, maybe with some small responsibility.
- Get someone in the cell to look after them.
- Share with the person, privately, the vision for cell life.
- Pray for God to break in.
- Ask if they would host the group.

So in summary…

- Give ownership to the group at every opportunity.
- Adopt a non-teaching style of leadership.
- Encourage contributions from the group.
- Affirm members at all times.
- Explain what is happening in order to create security in the group.
- Use body language to encourage contribution.
- Use repetition to emphasise what God has been saying to the group.
- Listen positively and use helpful questions.
- Keep the pace through the meeting.
- Start on time.
- Ensure individuals don't dominate the group.
- Don't set yourself up as the expert.

Safety

The joy of a small group is it can become a safe place. A sense of community develops, a bonding which means that 'what happens in the group stays in the group'. If people participate and their participation is a bit out of order or not on track, it doesn't matter. This is a safe place. Laugh or cry, get it right, get it wrong, these are friends. No judgements passed, all participation welcome.

Questions for discussion

Ask the group to share their experiences of working with people, and how the ideas shared here will help them in future?

Which of the ideas will you find most challenging to implement, and why?

Chapter 6
Supporting small group leaders

Welcome question
Share an example of when you have experienced someone's support.

Section 1 (40 mins)

So what will help?

We all need others to help us to do well and thrive. This is certainly true when it comes to leading a small group. It is a fact that many small group leaders feel unsupported and often describe what they do in leading a small group as unappreciated by the larger church and sadly sometimes the central church leadership.

Small groups are often the hidden engine of the church, helping their members grow and develop behind the scenes and enabling them to live effectively for Jesus in every area of their lives. But the small group leaders may not get the support and focus of central leadership that more public areas of church life receive. So we have to think about giving this area our attention along with other aspects and ensure that the leaders are equipped and supported so they and their groups can thrive and flourish.

We need to recognise that this idea of supporting small group leaders has not been part of our thinking in some churches so patterns and ideas around this will be new to some. With this in mind it is important that we understand not only how this might work but why it is important.

Keeping the groups linked to the life of the larger church

As we have already discussed, one description of church life is as the big wing and the small group wing. This gives a picture of a bird that can fly with two wings in motion together. The two wings need to be joined together to work effectively and enable flight. There is a danger that these two wings get separated and can even appear in competition with each other. With this in mind we need to look at how they can remain connected and indeed what connects them?

One of the connections from the small groups to the larger body of the church is that the bible section of the small group is based on the Sunday teaching from the main church. This keeps things on track and encourages the groups to be working with the same issues that arise from the content of Sundays and in doing so provides cohesion across the life of the church as a whole. The idea here is not that the sermon is re preached in each group but that the content is explored and most importantly applied to our lives. We looked at how this works in Chapter 4.

Coaching

A second connection, which we have already touched on, often comes in the form of a coach or support person for the group and its leader. This can happen in a number of ways so we will explore a few here and you can work with whatever suits your situation or is appropriate in your particular church culture.

Relationship vs role

As we think about how you as a small group leader will be supported it is helpful for us to look at some of the areas that may be covered. We have put this under the heading of 'relationship vs role' because, as small group leaders, we can perhaps feel intimidated or that we are being checked up on by someone who is really there as a coach to help us thrive in our leadership of a small group. So, to understand the way that we work together in terms of relationship and building a supportive friendship rather than perhaps focusing on the role or title of the individual who is with us, can be helpful.

One of the keys to supporting small group leaders is developing a coaching and supportive relationship. This comes out of having the role of being a coach for them but that is not the overriding driver. You need to be in this as a friend and confidant not just because you have signed up to take on the role of coach. With this in mind, here are a few areas to look at as you meet up.

The first is 'how are they doing in the whole of life?' So ask about work and family time commitments etc. and their general wellbeing as you would with any good friendship. This starts you off on the right foot as far as putting relationship above role is concerned. Working in this way values the person you are meeting with as a whole person rather than just as a volunteer in a role. This sits comfortably with the New Testament's emphasis on us being in relationships that are described in terms of family, using the language of brother and sister.

Secondly, it is good to talk about spiritual life and ask how they are connecting with God. It is vital that those who are leading our small groups have a dynamic and living relationship with Jesus. This is not to say that everything has to be sorted in this respect as we all have seasons in our lives where our relationship with God is not as buoyant as we would like it to be. A pattern of personal prayer and bible study should be part of a small group leader's diet to enable them to lead out of a place of connection with God. This will vary in style and frequency with each person but is an area that is often not talked about and kept private, so to initiate conversations around it in a supportive way is essential. Using open questions is helpful in this area so 'how would you describe your relationship with God at the moment' may be a good starter. As with any relationship it is imperative that we listen actively and give time to allow them to answer as fully as possible.

Thirdly, we need to focus on the group they are leading. We can do this in a number of ways. Firstly, in general about how the group is working in terms of personalities and any issues that may arise from group dynamics. Also, how individuals are developing in themselves and anything of concern to the leader about specific situations that have arisen (we will talk more about this in a later section). Another area we will want to explore is areas where their leadership might be developed. This can be ascertained through gentle questioning around areas that are working well and those that are perhaps a bit of a struggle. For instance, some small group leaders find it challenging to give parts of the meeting away to group members and need to be encouraged to take risks in this area and not hold on to their leadership too tightly. This may come to light as they describe that they are overwhelmed with making everything happen and preparing the meeting takes so much of their time. Some leaders struggle with the organisational side of the group and getting to grips with the details of who is going to do what and when. Many groups have one of the members act as an organiser which is their strength and this enables them to make a contribution to the group out of their gifting.

This highlights another area that it is worth mentioning at this point, which is that having a core group within each small group is often helpful. This is simply two or three of the group who are on page with you and can be relied on to help make it work. Identifying these individuals and helping the leaders to work with them in an informal way really helps to share the leadership.

A vital part of the role of a coach is to provide support for the leaders of the group. This can come in different ways at different times across the lifespan of the group.

In the beginning, as the group leadership is finding its way and the group is settling in and getting to know one another it is important to help those leading to feel confident in what they have undertaken and to assure them that you are available to chat and pray if necessary. As the group moves on things settle in a bit and a rhythm and pattern is established for the group, people start to get to know each other. There is a need to start asking slightly more in-depth questions and learning to trust each other. This takes the group forward and the group leadership needs to sense that this needs to happen and step out and indeed take a lead in being more open and creating trust. This can make them feel quite vulnerable and can be a bit unsettling for the group. In this space it is good to spend time alongside the leaders encouraging them to stay in the reality of this and not settle for surface relationships but continue to build the community of the group by going deeper in the relationships.

Another dimension of this shift to more reality in the group is sometimes a testing of the leadership; challenges are brought by some of the members to see if the leadership is really up to the job! This quite naturally unsettles the leaders and they need support and encouragement through this period. This is particularly true where a new way of running the group is being tried, or there is an expectancy that the group will have different outcomes or be run out of different values to previous groups. Explanation here is really helpful as understanding that this sort of thing is part of the development of group life depersonalises it to a degree. All this means spending time with the leaders through the process.

Questions for discussion

Describe how you feel about talking with a leader around the three areas mentioned above?

Which of the connections between the larger church and small groups are important for you and why?

Section 2 (20mins)

Challenging situations

Many small groups struggle because they have challenging situations that revolve around particular individuals either on an ongoing basis or for a particular season of an individual's life. We all have challenging moments in our lives often when pain in one form or another comes and knocks on our door. Small groups are very good at supporting individuals through these seasons with not only prayer but often practical help as well. Where the groups have the sort of atmospheres that we described earlier of honesty and participation then things are more likely to come to light, and we need to be prepared to work with what comes up.

However, as mentioned briefly in Chapter 3 we need to recognise that in some situations people need more support than the group can offer. This is particularly true where a situation is ongoing and sometimes true where a crisis has emerged that needs shorter term input of a more professional nature. Where this is the case a pathway needs to be in place so the small group leader can talk to a member of the central leadership team about their concerns and referral can be offered to an appropriate agency. In less demanding situations, some support from a member of the church outside of the small group can be offered. In either situation it is helpful that action is taken as soon as a situation is recognised, both for the sake of the individual and to ensure that the group does not become over burdened trying to offer unrealistic ongoing support.

Each church will differ in response to these situations and have particular systems in place to enable discipleship and pastoral care; the key here is to be clear about how this works and who needs to be involved. In most situations the earlier something is highlighted the better.

Questions for discussion

What systems are in place to offer support in your church situation and how are they accessed?

Section 3 (30 mins)

Being part of a team

It is important for many small group leaders to know that they are part of a team of other leaders who are also running small groups. This gives a sense of shared ownership of this part of the church's life and stops those leading feeling as if they are out there doing it alone. To this end there are a number of things that can create this sense of team. Here we explore further some of the ideas mentioned in Chapter 3, which you might like to consider:

Gather small group leaders for ongoing training. This can be in your own setting or indeed joining the regular training sessions run by Cell UK. Topics to look at can be sought from the leaders themselves if you are planning to run the training yourself as they often have an idea of where they would appreciate more input.

Gather small group leaders for feedback and prayer. A number of churches do this on a Sunday evening or over a Saturday morning breakfast. This often involves hearing from each group about how the last few weeks have been. It is a good place to feed back on how the Sunday morning teaching has been applied in the groups and issues that have come up that may need addressing in a future teaching series. It is also a place to hear how other groups are doing and share good practice and ideas that have worked well in other groups whether they be around worship, outreach etc. This cross pollination builds strong sense of team amongst the leaders as they encourage and support each other in sharing ideas.

An awayday or weekend. This can have a mixture of content covering such areas as worshipping and praying together, having some teaching input and time for revitalisation and refreshment. **Giving space for conversations and fun activities together.** Out for a walk, a few board games a creative activity etc. All this builds team and gives a context for support and relationships to develop.

Involving this group in the decision making process of the life of the church. Some churches see their small group leaders as part of an extended leadership team. This often happens in an informal way but is invaluable as this group of leaders are often in touch with insights and feelings of the members of their groups that are helpful to bring to the table. Also these leaders can carry a sense of vision from the centre of the church into their small groups so a two way flow can happen here.

Questions for discussion

What are the benefits of being part of a team?

How does your church gather the leaders of small groups?

Chapter 7
Small group evangelism
Laurence Singlehurst reflects

Welcome question
Who most influenced you to follow Jesus and how did it happen?

Section 1 (30 mins)

Missional Heartbeat

There comes a moment in one's mission activities when you realize that something so simple and yet profound has been missing. In 1995, I wrote a book called Sowing, Reaping, Keeping, which I'm pleased to say is still in print and is seen by many to be a fundamental book on understanding mission and evangelism in today's context.

In 2003, the publisher asked me to re-write the book and update it. In doing that, I took the opportunity to pray a prayer that was basically just being polite. The prayer was that if there was anything fundamentally wrong in the original book (but of course there wasn't), that the good Lord might let me know. I had plenty of new material, so I began to write. The more I wrote, the more uneasy I became. I began to feel that God was speaking to me about the original book and that there was a significant problem with it. My immediate response to this was 'Are you sure God? Have you read it?' Eventually a metaphor came to mind: you can take a horse to the water, but if it is not thirsty, it won't drink. I felt the Holy Spirit began to speak to me that mission is not a structure or programme, mission is about a question. The question is 'How big is your heart?'

John 3:16 does not say 'God so hated the world that he sent his son to judge it', but God so LOVED the world. In other words, mission began in God's heart. Out of that love came action, the sending of his son. I realize that in many ways I have spent 20 years trying to encourage people into mission, either by preaching in big meetings, or by pushing the subject in small meetings. Up to a point this does encourage individuals, but when you stop that encouragement, churches often stop reaching out. Mission begins in the heart. If we can all have a heart change then the structure becomes a vehicle to support what we want to do from our heart motivation. With a heart change we begin to understand the real nature of loving the world.

In thinking about this, I tried to find a metaphor that helps us understand that mission begins in the heart. I was reminded of some words that Ed Silvoso wrote. He encouraged every Christian to think of themselves as a pastor, but their congregation was made up of those outside the church from their community. We should do the two things a good pastor does; love people unconditionally regardless of whether they respond or not and yet seek their spiritual welfare. I began to see that I needed to have a small group of people that I belonged to, and that my small group's role was to pray for me to have a big heart and to empower me to love my unchurched congregation.

Shortly after this thought, my friend Bob invited me to join his darts club, which met in a small garage. The first night I went, I realized I'd forgotten what it felt like to be in a relatively small room where the other six people smoked, and my wife and I did not. By the end of the night, I thought I was going to die. In reflecting back to the Lord, I said I was very happy to be a pastor, but was it possible for me to have a non-smoking congregation? I felt God opened the doors of heaven and looked down and said 'Poor Laurence. Is the smokey wokie getting up your nosey wosie?' Then I thought that perhaps hanging on a cross was not such a good experience, and if Jesus could hang on a cross for me, then I could be a member of this group. For ten years, most Thursday nights, I sat in this group with my good friends. How will people know about the love of God unless in some way we connect with them.

I learnt that in beginning a small group, before we put mission on the agenda, we need to reflect together how easy or how hard it is to make friends or to serve in a project. We need to ask God to give us the right motivation - for a big heart. Week by week as we think about those we are reaching out to, we pray not only for them, but we pray for ourselves that our hearts would be big and we would be motivated by love.

Mission in our context

I think we all understand that the culture of this nation has gone through a radical change. It is no longer a secular nation where legislation sits on a Christian moral foundation. We are a secular nation with roots in post-modernism. It is a totally different culture - not all bad, not all good, just different. Just as the culture has changed, so mission needs to change if it is going to make a connection with the new culture. So what are some of those big changes?

Firstly, we have become a culture where belief in 'one truth' is no longer accepted. We have become cynical about politicians, church leaders or anyone who claims to have the truth. We are a culture who wants to see before we believe. We want to touch it and see it before we believe it and if we can touch it and see it, then we might be prepared to listen to the truth which lies behind what we have seen. This of course is the Jesus way. Jesus came and lived amongst people. He was one of us. He was totally and fully connected. He encouraged them to come, to follow, to see and to experience. When the disciples of John came and asked him 'Are you the one?' He told them to tell John what they had seen and experienced.

As the church, we need to learn to walk a different way. In times past, because of the love and service of previous generations, many understood and accepted the gospel as truth often before they experienced much of the Christian community of love and action. But in today's society we must put love first. We must connect and demonstrate how we live out our Christian faith before we earn the right to speak. We are not ashamed of words, but recognize both their power and limitations.

What does this look like? Jesus told his disciples in Matthew 28 to go and make disciples. In modern English we could say that we are to be authentic and to be connected. Contextual mission, in my mind, looks like these two things. It is about being authentic whole-life disciples seeking to demonstrate Christ in and through every aspect of our lives. It looks like empowered people who connect to their world through friendship, love and service, in the context of where they work and where they live. This is our front line.

I think that in the past I overemphasized the power of friendship evangelism, thinking everybody could make friends and just be hospitable. I now see that is not the case. It simply is not enough. We must demonstrate love by being as personally relational as we can, joining sports clubs, interest groups, being a good neighbour, being hospitable. All of these things we can do as individuals. We also recognize that to connect truly we must serve our communities using our creativity and local knowledge to meet local needs. The Cinnamon Network *(www.cinnamonnetwork.co.uk)* have identified twenty seven simple ideas that local churches could do that demonstrate unconditional love for their community. Amongst their suggestions are starting a food bank, helping people with their debts, visiting the housebound, giving lunch to young people in the holidays who may be hungry or helping people with addictions. These projects have given churches a whole new confidence. Our small groups empower people to friendship and to service. As we do more of these projects, we will need more people and more people will come to serve and be a part because their small groups empower, support and encourage them to do so.

Questions for discussion

Why is loving people part of our outreach?

Share a situation where your heart has been changed towards someone and describe the circumstances that enabled it to happen.

Section 2 (30 mins)

Some practicalities

I believe that the first stage of our mission today is connection, and this demonstrates unconditional love through friendship or service as we have just discussed. We might discover through this connection where people are in their experience of God.

The second stage is to offer people an opportunity to hear the words. This could be a step into spiritual interest and on to understanding the content of the spiritual message. This is where small groups and church structures need to work together in partnership.

Here are some ways that this could come about and the part a small group could play in it.

Becoming comfortable to talk about spiritual things

Being part of a small group that enables participation is one way of getting people used to talking about their relationship with God. In the past this has often been the area in which only leaders voices are heard. So as different people in the group voice what it is like for them to have a relationship with God then language is developed and concepts are formed for them. This makes it easier for them to answer questions when asked about their faith in an everyday context.

An individual sharing their personal story, why they believe

Using a welcome question in a small group like: 'How did you first come to know Jesus?' gives group members an opportunity to tell their story in a safe place. This builds confidence and allows them to see how parts of their journey of faith fit together. This can also be a good place to look at some of the objections people raise to believing in God and how we can talk about these in a helpful way. So we may ask a welcome question about what we would say if someone asked us how we know Jesus is real.

Learning to listen for where people are on their spiritual journey

One of the other skills we develop in a small group that encourages participation is an ability to listen to each other, this sounds obvious but it is a key area which relates to the way we think about mission. In a world where people are approaching faith from such different backgrounds and perspectives we need to develop good listening skills and discernment of where they are and what it might be helpful for us to talk to them about.

Making relevant and helpful connections to Jesus

Bringing Jesus into our everyday conversations, again this sounds obvious but all too often I don't think we do this naturally. So once again, our small group can help us out here. Encouraging our group members to talk about how they interact with Jesus throughout the week is one way of starting this. This does two things: it gets us reflecting on how and when this happens and also gets us used to sharing these stories with each other so this becomes a more natural thing for us. We can then consider sharing some of these examples with friends and work colleagues as the occasion arises, and in particular when they ask us questions about the practicalities of our faith.

Making connections to the Jesus story

Another idea and good way to create lively content for our small group and help us in our outreach as individuals is to look at the stories about Jesus that we each resonate with. All of us have our favourite story about Jesus, one that we connect with and has particular meaning for us. Many of these stories are not now common currency in our culture. So it's a good idea for us to be able to tell them. The telling of these stories is especially powerful because they have a significance to us personally and our retelling of them and why we like them bring them to life in a whole new way. So we can do this in our small group and give encouragement to one another and perhaps take the opportunity to share them with our friends when the opportunity arises.

Invitations

If you are like me, you are full of good intentions but need help to deliver these intentions in real terms. I often imagine people that I could invite to various things. However it takes some sort of external pressure to help me do what I want to. My small group has been good in this regard as I share what I would like to do, i.e. invite my neighbours to sing carols in our street before Christmas. The group can then ask me how I am doing with it and offer to turn up and bring mulled wine and make it happen! In this way we can help each other do the things that we have a heart to do.

Resources

We are often a bit private about our faith and find it helpful to have something we can give to our friends. Lending them a book, DVD etc. is one way of doing this and stirring spiritual interest and seeking their feedback about what they have read or watched. Again, looking at this in our small groups can be really encouraging, as we can share the resources that we have found helpful and we could give to others. We can then pray for each other and our friends as we give them out.

Being real

There is a need for us to be real about the challenges we face as Christians and share the things that we are struggling with as well as the good news. Authenticity is a very strong felt need in our society and so we need to be vulnerable and share those parts of our faith that we are grappling with. Again our small groups should be places of authenticity and honesty so to have those conversations here will help us to be real with our friends in our everyday world. I think doing this is very attractive and there are plenty of biblical examples of this so we are in good company.

The last stage, stage three of this relational pathway might be an invitation to discover what it means to be a Christian, maybe through Alpha, or to encourage people to pray and talk to God for themselves. I have done some informal research over the years and have found that over 30% of British people have made their most meaningful step to God on their own.

Our small groups enable us to be authentic, real disciples. Whether through friendship or through a project, people can see that we are real, although not perfect. They can see something of our faith and that we are connected to people. Through these connections we offer people a spiritual journey. We will love them regardless of whether they take the journey or not, but we are not ashamed to offer them that possibility.

I think the question being asked by our non Christian friends has changed. Once they asked 'is it true?' The world was structured around objective truth and our reality was being expressed in this way. As our culture has become more post modern and experiential, the question has become 'does it work?'. This is the reason why we need to live differently so people can see that being a Christian makes a difference and then they might consider whether it is true.

Questions for discussion

Which of the ideas above are most attractive to you and why?

What do you think about the shift from objective truth to experiential encounter?

Section 3 (30 mins)

The challenge we face

There are a number of areas we need to think about when it comes to effective evangelism and numerical church growth. Firstly, there is no doubt that the soil in which we are sowing the seeds of the gospel in the UK is not as fertile as it is in other parts of the world.

Secondly, we have not been engaging with our communities and changing their perspectives until quite recently. Thirdly, we have used confrontational methods of evangelism in a culture that no longer really believes in truth and the power of words. Fourthly, some of the words we often use are no longer in general parlance, words like sin, repent, born again. There has been a communication problem with people not understanding what we are saying. Fifthly, the power of consumerism, the hedonism of our culture, the pursuit of pleasure and the avoidance of pain is proving to be an extremely powerful barrier. In Cell UK we have concluded that groups are always going to grow more slowly here in the UK.

Another area we have needed to look at is the way in which small groups multiply. The idea of these holistic small groups emerged in the UK a year or two after Alpha had begun. This was a significant game changer. It is my contention that because of Alpha and because of a particularly British characteristic, our groups were never going to multiply in the same way as in other countries. Groups in Singapore and South America mainly grew on the basis of personal evangelism. Individuals were mobilized, they reached out to their friends, led those friends to Christ and brought them into their small group. The group grew and had to multiply.

However, here in the UK, despite a hundred years of encouragement, British people do not ask personal or leading questions. Whereas we are happy to share our story and our faith with our friends, it is perhaps a cultural step too far, an invasion of private space, to ask them a leading question. We would much prefer to ask them to do something where someone else puts up the proposition or brings a challenge. In the past, that opportunity was provided by gospel meetings or guest services.

What we quickly perceived was happening in the UK was that members of these holistic small groups had been mobilized, they did reach out to their friends. They invited their friends to Alpha, their friends came to faith in that process and new groups were started at the end of Alpha. We discovered that on the whole the small group idea was more successful than we had thought. Local churches who embraced this idea had seen growth primarily as the fruit of Alpha. People were on an Alpha course because they met an individual who was mobilized and supported through their small group, who was able to invite them to Alpha.

One spin off from this was that, rather than the groups getting bigger, they sometimes got smaller. They sent some of their key group members to sit at the Alpha table who then became leaders of new small groups.

One or two churches followed a slightly different route. An existing small group became the host of an Alpha course which looked a little bit like a classic small group meeting, except there was a meal instead of an icebreaker, followed by the Alpha talk and discussion. Later on the whole group attended the 'Holy Spirit' weekend. When some of the people on the Holy Spirit weekend came to faith, they stayed within the group which then needed to multiply in that classic sense.

Some churches have had groups which did multiply. This happened through folding in existing church members and adding some who had become Christians. However the lesson we have learnt is that the real gift of the small group is that it mobilizes people; it empowers them to be missional; it holds them accountable to whether they are making friends outside the church, whether they are holding hands with these friends through their loving service. I believe it creates a steady stream of people into church through Alpha and their guest services. In that sense we see that small groups in the UK have been successful in as much as the hard ground allows. The good news is that the perception of Christians and of church is being changed as more and more Christians get involved in loving service, in friendship, in projects, going out into the world as a mobilized workforce. It is this changed perception that leads to a greater openness to the gospel. My belief is that if we persist in church in the big and the small, and in love and service, we will see increasing numbers of people coming to faith as there is greater spiritual openness.

Supporting people on their front line

Mark Greene, Executive Director of The London Institute for Contemporary Christianity *(www.licc.org.uk)*, has championed the thought that 'everyone is a full-time Christian worker'. A cry for, 'whole life discipleship'. Small groups can help deliver this. One example of the way this happens is where in turn each member of the group shares what they do from Monday to Friday. They outline the joys they live with, the challenges that they face, and they ask the group to pray for them.

This can be a very powerful time as the group gather round a group member and lift them to God in prayer. This can be done by focusing on one person each week. It does not take the whole meeting time but just needs twenty minutes or so. This helps to break down the sacred/secular divide and connects the whole group with the reality of living out our Christian faith in the real world. It affirms each of us as full time Christian workers being salt and light in the whole of life.

Questions for discussion

In what ways do you anticipate people will come to faith in your setting?

What part will small groups play in the above?

Chapter 8
Experiencing life in a small group

We have discovered over many years that one of the ways people learn is through experience. A biblical example of this is in Romans 12:1-2:

> *'Therefore, I urge you, brothers and sisters, in view of God's mercy, to offer your bodies as a living sacrifice, holy and pleasing to God—this is your true and proper worship. ² Do not conform to the pattern of this world, but be transformed by the renewing of your mind. Then you will be able to test and approve what God's will is—his good, pleasing and perfect will.'*

We often focus on verse two about the transforming of our minds, however the context for this mind change is set in verse one, where we see that we need to offer our bodies as 'living sacrifices which is our spiritual worship'. So, it is in the context of our experience, through offering our bodies as living sacrifices that our minds are transformed. From this perspective we are offering three small group outlines in this chapter so you can run a small group and reflect on your experiences. We have also included some reflection questions, by using these you can consolidate your learning together.

The outlines are based around the very popular 4Ws format, which we think of as being like a garden trellis in that its purpose is to help the plants to grow rather than be on display in its own right.

The individual sections that form the welcome, worship, word and witness, are taken from some of our resources so you can see how they work in this context and we have referenced them for your convenience.

We suggest that a different person from the group acts as the facilitative leader each week and that each section of the group is given away so that everyone has a chance to lead at least one section over the three weeks. It may be helpful for each member of the group to have a copy of our booklet *Help I am leading part of my small group'* (available from celluk.org.uk) as this gives background information about how to make the different sections of the group work well and highlights some of the things that it is good to prepare beforehand.

We suggest that you spend some time at the end of each meeting talking together about how it went, what you observed and what each of you who participated by leading part of the meeting discovered as you lead.

It will be helpful to see how the pattern of the evening outworks the beliefs and values that we looked at earlier so here is a simple chart that shows how these are brought to life through the 4Ws format:

Structure	Belief	Value
Welcome	God loves and values us	All involved/creating community
Worship	Loving God	Encountering God
Word	Loving one another	Becoming disciples
Witness	Loving our lost world	Doing evangelism

Week 1

The theme for this week is: Encourage one another

Welcome

Who is influencing you and what are you learning from them?

Taken from: Discipleship deck card, available from celluk.org.uk

Worship

Theme: Life giving water

Preparation: requires a bowl, jug of water and a towel.

Place a bowl and a jug of water along with a towel in the centre of the room.

Ask someone to read John 4:13-14 where Jesus speaks to the woman at the well about life giving water:

Jesus answered, 'Everyone who drinks this water will be thirsty again, but whoever drinks the water I give them will never thirst. Indeed, the water I give them will become in them a spring of water welling up to eternal life.'

As the verses are read, take the jug and pour the water out into the bowl slowly and deliberately.

Take time to then wash each other's hands in the bowl, praying as you do that God will refresh your lives again as you do this together.

Taken from: 40 more Creative worship ideas, available from celluk.org.uk

Word

Hebrews 10:23-25

'Let us hold unswervingly to the hope we profess, for he who promised is faithful. And let us consider how we may spur one another on toward love and good deeds, not giving up meeting together, as some are in the habit of doing, but encouraging one another—and all the more as you see the Day approaching.'

Thoughts from this passage

No one likes a 'moaning Minnie' (as my Mum calls them) or the Eeyore's of this world as A. A. Milne characterises them. We can easily find ourselves drawn into rather negative conversations that pull us and others down. Picking holes in people or situations seems to be a regular pastime for many. These verses ask us to do something completely different. As Christians we are called to be people of hope, people who believe in a God of the possible where change and redemption are real possibilities. One of the things I love about small groups is that they can be places of real encouragement where we can spur one another on as we seek to follow Jesus in our everyday lives.

Like most of the 'one anothers' in the New Testament, this is set firmly in the context of a small group where open relationships and support can be fostered. The hope in these verses is not based on anything we might have done or plan to do, but on what God has done, 'for he who promised is faithful'.

A friend once described my own gift of encouragement as a bit like 'a poke with a sharp stick!' A prod to action you might say. A deliberate attempt to get someone to do something that they may be a little reluctant to do, but which will ultimately be good for them and those around them. In this way we are stimulating courage in those that we seek to encourage.

Questions
What are these 'love and good deeds' that these verses focus on? Are you drawn to particular sorts of loving and good deeds?

When did you last experience a 'poke with a sharp stick?' What was the outcome?

We all receive encouragement in different ways. How would it be helpful for members of your group to encourage you?

Response
Share current situations where you feel you are in need of encouragement.

What would you like the Lord to help you with? Ask for his encouragement and notice the encouragement that comes in all sorts of creative ways between now and when you next meet as a group. Remember to give feedback next time you meet.

Also think of areas where you could encourage others this coming week, make sure these are genuine and thoughtful. Notice the difference it makes.

Taken from: Encounter, 20 interactive Bible studies for small groups, available from celluk.org.uk

Witness

Using our talents
Read the parable of the talents together from Matthew 25:14–30 perhaps read round the group, one verse each.

It is often difficult for us to see what talents God has given us. It can be more obvious to others. Spend a few minutes sharing with each other the things that you see God has given each of you as gifts in your character or skills.

Talk about how these can be used more effectively as we share our faith with others and discover through your conversations how each of you will do this slightly differently because of your gifts.

Pray prayers of thanks for the gifts you have unearthed together and bless one another as you do so.

Taken from: 40 Missional ideas for small groups, available from celluk.org.uk

ial life in a small group

Week 2

The theme for this week is: Making the most of every opportunity

Welcome

How would your non-Christian friends describe you?

Taken from: Discipleship deck card, available from celluk.org.uk

Worship

Theme: Our story

Requires no preparation: other than the bible.

Set the scene by reminding the group that the bible is made up of stories of people's encounters with God down through history.

Read the story of Zacchaeus in Luke 19:1-10.

Explain that we are going to take a few moments to share our stories briefly with each other, focusing on our encounters with Jesus. This could be a recent encounter or how we first met Jesus. Go round the group and in no more than two minutes each take it in turns to share your Jesus story.

Spend time thanking God in prayer for each other's stories

Taken from: 40 more Creative worship ideas, available from celluk.org.uk

Word

Colossians 4:2-6

'Devote yourselves to prayer, being watchful and thankful. And pray for us, too, that God may open a door for our message, so that we may proclaim the mystery of Christ, for which I am in chains. Pray that I may proclaim it clearly, as I should. Be wise in the way you act toward outsiders; make the most of every opportunity. Let your conversation be always full of grace, seasoned with salt, so that you may know how to answer everyone.'

Thoughts from this passage

Have you ever explained something to someone and detected that they have not understood it - maybe a practical task at work, an instruction to a child or in conversation with your spouse? It is surely a common occurrence for many of us. As it is often said, communication is a two way thing. There is a deliverer and a receiver. Paul knew this and asked for prayer in both the delivery and reception of his vital message. His phrase 'open a door for our message' has the receiver as its focus, 'pray that I may proclaim it clearly' has the deliverer in mind.

It is good to recognise that we are not alone in our struggle to speak to people about the love of God. We are indeed in good company if the apostle Paul found this a challenge and asked others to pray for him. Let's be real about this. At this time in our culture we meet few who are ready and open to hear our traditional message. We have to earn the right to speak about the God we know by demonstrating authentic, unconditional love, usually over a long period, before we can break down the stereotypes of Christians. We have to understand the messages in our culture so we can speak in a way that is relevant and helpful. Perhaps our message needs to come from a different angle than when we heard it and responded. Paul found ways of speaking about God in each of the places he visited. He used his own story but with a cultural bias to capture the attention of those he spoke to. Also he made sure he was wise in the way he acted toward outsiders in order to make the most of every opportunity. He suggests that we let our conversation be always full of grace, seasoned with salt, so that you may know how to answer everyone.

Questions
How should we speak about God in our culture? What is relevant to our friends and contacts? Does the message of sin and redemption still communicate?

Where are the open doors or slightly open doors for our message in our situation?

What might be the reason for people not being open?

Response
How can we be confident that our encounters will always be full of grace? What do these conversations that are 'seasoned with salt' mean to you?

How does fear hold you back from speaking? Explore together what stops you making the most of every opportunity or perhaps even creating opportunities.

If your group is ready then pray for each other both for opportunities to share the gospel but also skill to do that clearly and well. Take a few moments to allow each person in the group to bring someone to mind who they may have an opportunity to share with.

Commit to being more open to hearing God this coming week and make plans to share about situations where you have encountered him next time you meet together.

Taken from: Encounter, 20 interactive Bible studies for small groups, available from celluk.org.uk

Witness

Jesus stories

Laurence suggests that one way for ordinary church members to share their faith is to talk about Jesus. Around the world there is a growing momentum behind the realisation that putting Jesus forward is the best evangelism we can do today.

People are surprisingly ignorant of what Jesus said and did. This means that our 'Jesus stories' come across with a freshness and a power. Ask the members of the small group to think of a story about Jesus in the Gospels that has been meaningful and impacted them personally. Ask people to think how they might retell that particular incident or story and how they might explain its personal resonance to someone else. Trial run some of these stories in your small group. You could ask one or two people each week to share one of their favourite Jesus stories from the Gospels. Pray for one another as you look for opportunities to share these stories with your friends.

An example of such a story can be found at www.celluk.org.uk/jesusstories

Taken from: 40 Missional ideas for small groups, available from celluk.org.uk

Week 3

The theme for this week is: Self image

Welcome

If you could live one moment of your life all over again which one would it be?

Taken from: Icebreaker playing cards, available from celluk.org.uk

Worship

Preparation: Requires items from nature.

Bring an item from the natural world (flower, rock, fossil, feather, piece of wood etc). Place the item or items in a prominent place so that everyone can see them.

Read Genesis 1 together, take a verse each and go round the group to encourage the whole group to engage with the passage.
Before you read together ask the group to reflect on the rhythm of the passage and notice the repeated phrases.

'God said'

'God saw that it was good'

'And there was evening and there was morning'

Use the items and the repeated phrases from the passage as your stimulus for prayer and worship together.

Taken from: 40 more Creative worship ideas, available from celluk.org.uk

Word

Romans 12:3

'For by the grace given me I say to every one of you: do not think of yourself more highly than you ought, but rather think of yourself with sober judgment, in accordance with the faith God has distributed to each of you.'

'Therefore, if anyone is in Christ, the new creation has come;'
2 Corinthians 5:17

Thoughts from this passage

In the 1950s Dr Maxwell Maltz, a well-known plastic surgeon, noticed that when he did plastic surgery it often had a very positive impact on his patients' self-image, their confidence and what they felt they could or could not do. The effect of the surgery seemed out of all proportion to the actual intervention. Later he discovered that by helping people to think positively about themselves he didn't always have to do surgery as people accepted what they looked like. This too had a profoundly positive impact on their confidence and what they could or could not do.

We know that today many of us suffer from a low self-image, feelings of low self-worth. These feelings can rob us of the motivation to do certain things, leading sometimes to all sorts of negative and destructive behaviours. Psychologists say that these feelings are so powerful that they form a script, a repetitive message, which can control us in a negative way.

Rather than imagining yourself to be one of the beautiful, successful people so applauded in our world, how about imagining yourself receiving the loving gaze of God? What does he say about me? I am not the outcome of my successes and failures, my life's experience, but he sees me as his creation which he said was good.

He couldn't love and accept me more than he does right now.

Questions

What is it that transforms the way we feel about ourselves? Is it being told that we are new creations or that we should think of ourselves with sober judgement - both of which are true - or something else?

What has been your experience of learning to love and accept yourself?

What would become possible if you could live from a deep knowledge of being loved and accepted?

Response

In learning to receive love, it is as if a light has been shone into our lives, revealing both goodness and the things in the shadows. How can we support each other as we journey with our shadow side; our fears, our shame and our anger?

A Prayer

'Father, I recognise that I am more than who my background says I am. I am not shaped by those negative things that have been said to me. I am a new creation, created and loved by you. Help me not to avoid my shadow side, but to have the courage to face those things which stop me from receiving your love and living as you would want me to.'

Taken from: Encounter, 20 interactive Bible studies for small groups, available from celluk.org.uk

Witness

Luke 10:2 – praying

In Luke 10:2 we are told 'the harvest is plentiful pray therefore for the labourers,' i.e. the workers. Many times when we think of being missional, we think of praying for our colleagues at work or our neighbours but this scripture encourages us to pray for ourselves because we are the workers.

Action: perhaps once a quarter during the year in our small group meetings we could take five minutes at the end and pray for one person around these questions:

1. What are the pressures you face in your workplace life as a Christian?

Let us pray that God would sustain them at work as we know that the work environment is more pressured than ever before and pray for them that they can love and value their colleagues.

2. Who are their friends in their local neighbourhood? Use the metaphor of 'whose hands are you holding' (shorthand for how many relational connections do you have) and pray for that person in the context of the local relationships that they may or may not have.

Taken from: 40 Missional ideas for small groups, available from celluk.org.uk

Other resources

Small Groups - an Introduction *Laurence Singlehurst*
This booklet seeks to give some biblical background and framework along with a practical understanding of what it might be like to part of a small group. Suitable for those joining or starting a group, or for those already in one to refresh your understanding of what it means to be in a small group.

Help! I'm Leading Part of my Small Group
Trevor Withers
Designed to help small group members who are leading one of the sections of the meeting on any occasion. The aim is to increase the understanding of what should be happening in each of the sections and give practical ideas and help that will make the section you are leading a success.

Encounter *Laurence Singlehurst and Trevor Withers*
Designed specifically for small groups, these Bible studies are interactive and participatory, and encourage application to everyday life. We hope that as small groups use these Bible studies they will indeed encounter the presence of God as they apply each lesson and pray for one another.

Discipleship Deck playing cards
We think this is a really good resource: it's a pack of 52 cards, each containing a question or challenge about relationships, lifestyle, spiritual growth or mission. These cards can be used in any discipleship context, but we think they also lend themselves exceedingly well to small groups. For example, some of the cards would make fantastic ice-breakers for the welcome section of your small group meeting, others would be very suitable for the witness section. And it makes it very easy for members to participate by leading one of the sections of your small group.

Other resources

40 more Creative Worship Ideas
After the success of our first set of Creative Worship Ideas our second set also cover a broad range of Christian worship. We all connect with God in different ways, so these sets of cards each contain a range of ideas with the hope that everyone in your group can lead worship confidently, as follows:
Our lives; Scripture; Objects; Words; The natural world; Games; 'I am' sayings of Jesus; Stories behind the hymns

40 Missional Ideas for Small Groups
How can each one of us live out Christ in the context of where we work, where we live and in our families? We have brought together 40 fantastic ideas for use in small groups. Each idea takes about fifteen minutes and gives practical ways to encourage and empower each other as we seek to love those around us and share Jesus with them. Printed on attractive postcards and presented in a high quality durable tin, these ideas break down into eight themes each taking your small group on a journey, renewing minds and creating new rhythms for life.

Sowing Reaping Keeping *Laurence Singlehurst*
This book will help us explore what it really means to love people and fulfil our responsibility to share what we believe. It is not full of technical terms and complicated methods but simply explores what it means to sow the seeds of faith, to reap the harvest and to nurture the fruit as it grows. Sow. Reap. Keep. *Study guide for groups also available.*

4Life *Mark Powley*
Want to go deeper with God or refresh your faith? 4Life is full of honesty, passion and humour, and seeks to give a solid foundation for practical Christian living today. The ingredients are simple; ten readings on your own, then an honest meeting with a trusted mentor. The journey in these pages will leave you changed.

Other resources

2000 Years of Small Groups: A history of cell ministry in the church
Joel Comiskey
In this fascinating book Joel Comiskey chronicles the small group or cell movement from Jesus all the way to the modern day. Comiskey highlights the strengths and weaknesses of these historical small group movements and applies principles to today's church.

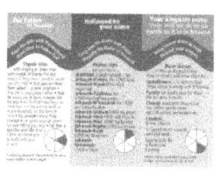

Prayer Cards
This is a dynamic way to use the Lord's Prayer and bring creative energy to your small group as you pray together. These cards can also be used by individuals in their own lives to give an effective pattern to their prayer life.

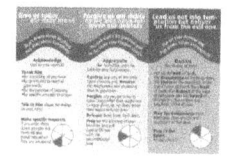

No rhythm of prayer has been more used, more loved and more appreciated over the centuries than The Lord's Prayer. This simple practical resource divides the prayer into bite-size sections; each card is laid out as 6 segments (double-sided i.e. 3 on each side) and gives creative ways to pray around each key phrase.

To purchase our books and resources and for information about our training days and courses visit our website at www.celluk.org.uk

Or phone: 01582 320565
email: cellukresources@oval.com

About the authors

Laurence Singlehurst

Laurence is the Director of Cell UK and was its founder over twenty years ago.

He has a passion for equipping churches to reach their communities, with an emphasis on friendship evangelism. He has a heart to see holistic small groups with a missional heartbeat established in churches up and down our nation.

He is also on the board and leadership team of HOPE, chairman of Westminster Theological College and a board member of several other charities.

He is a regular conference and church speaker.

Laurence is the author of several books including: the best seller Sowing Reaping Keeping, Loving the Lost, Beyond the Clouds and The Gospel Message Today.

Trevor Withers

Trevor helps to lead Cell UK and has been involved since its creation over 20 years ago. He is passionate about small groups and how they support us to live for Jesus in all of our lives.

He has worked with numerous churches from across the denominations and streams, has run training for small group leaders, and has created many small group and discipleship resources including Walking Together, Help I'm leading my Small Group, Encounter Bible Studies, Equipped to Lead, and Equipping future Cell Leaders.

Trevor also leads the leadership team of Network Church in St Albans which is part of the Pioneer group of Churches.

He has a heart for creativity and the arts and runs a pottery studio with a friend.

Lightning Source UK Ltd.
Milton Keynes UK
UKHW040622280119
336325UK00004B/27/P